Mine Eyes Have Seen: The American Dream Collection

Linda C. Thompson

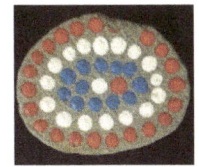

Published by New Generation Publishing in 2020

Copyright © Linda C. Thompson 2020

First Edition

The author asserts the moral right under the Copyright, Designs and Patents Act 1988 to be identified as the author of this work.

All Rights reserved. No part of this publication may be reproduced, stored in a retrieval system or transmitted, in any form or by any means without the prior consent of the author, nor be otherwise circulated in any form of binding or cover other than that which it is published and without a similar condition being imposed on the subsequent purchaser.

ISBN: 978-1-80031-923-3
Ebook ISBN: 978-1-80031-849-6

www.newgeneration-publishing.com

Cover photo by Michael A. Feit

Dedication

To Olympia, Daniel, Darcy and Walter for their inspiration, love and support.

"re-examine all you have been told in school or church or in any book, and dismiss whatever insults your own soul; and your very flesh shall be a great poem, and have the richest fluency, not only in its words, but in the silent lines of its lips and face, and between the lashes of your eyes, and in every motion and joint of your body."

[From the preface to Leaves Grass]
— **Walt Whitman, <u>Leaves of Grass</u>**

Contents

American Places

    Paradise Burning 8

    Beauty in Saratoga 14

    American City 18

    'Nawlins (New Orleans) 21

    New York City 27

    West Texas Day 29

    All You Have 31

    The Moment of America 34

American People

    OCAW 39

    Soldier's Poem 42

    Strip Mall Improvisation 45

    A Different Day 50

    Hey Baby 53

    Knuckles and Bone 57

    Robo Wolf 59

Nexus of Hearts 60

Street Prophets 62

Monarchs of the Drivers' Seat 66

Privileges of Citizenship 68

Kidz 71

Sunday Night Blues 73

We are American 74

American Soul

    American Dream 78

    America Dreaming 81

    American Spirits 84

    Balancing – City on a Hille 88

    From Whence We Came 90

    I Am My Own Country 92

    Strength of Your Muscles 93

    Color Song 95

    Mine Eyes Have Seen 100

    America blushed 113

    Epilogue 118

    Life in the Time of Pandemic 118

American Places

Paradise Burning

They came to Paradise
        Or Pair-o-dice
        Or Para dice
As all come
To marry, raise a family
Grow old and die…
To carve
"My own corner of Paradise,"
Peaceful, tucked in a canyon
In the mountains
Breezes creating pinesong…
Gentle summers
Modest winters
Hiking, fishing, picnics, arts and crafts
Perpetual family vacation.
Paradise, secret shared
Friendly wave
A smile, a nod
Tilt of the head, twinkling eyes

"We made it…

Paradise on earth

Just for us…"

Till Campfire…

Cruelest irony

Campfire…

Marshmallows

    Laughter

        Stories

            Music

Tiny embers

Falling like gracenotes,

Curious stares

Warnings beginning

TV and radio

Then…

Fire!

Leaping by football fields

Devouring

Great gaping fiery

Maw.

Exploding

Buildings

      Houses

            Cars

                   People

Breathless, choking, gasping

Flight

Flames licking along the roads

Threatening tires

Heat HEAT **HEAT!**

Gulping

Trying to stay awake

Sleep is death

Hiding the kids eyes

Burning skeletons slumped in cars

Smoke

Thick and solid

Owning space

Endless tunnel

Praying

      For the road

      To get through

      For breath

Terror like teeth and claws

Seconds were hours

Somehow -
Firefighters
Forming a line
Against the fire
Signaling
Drivers into parking lots
Air, water
Out of the car
Tears, hysteria
Holding each other tightly
Swaying, cradling, rocking
Breathing
    Breathing
        Breathing
Air is food
    Feeding
        Feeding
            Feeding.

It started on a Thursday in November
By Sunday
Only smoldering twisted shapes
86 dead
Few remains.

The souls,
The survivors…
Some returned, rebuilt
Most scattered
Someplace, anyplace
A few still float
Aimless
Blown like ash
Volition
Lost to the flames.

"…for now, the thought
Both of lost happiness and lasting pain
Torments him;"
John Milton, *Paradise Lost,* published 1667

Beauty in Saratoga

Saratoga in August
Comes alive
With the rich and the famous and the notorious.

Beautiful horses and patchwork people
Spend and Spend and Spend.
The horses spend their all on the track
People…well…you already know how and what people spend.

The most beautiful woman I have seen in Saratoga
Was ancient and alone in her very soul
In a cheap diner eating a turkey sandwich
Alone.

Entering, I stopped in my tracks.
Thoughts of the Ladies Room were misty
Compared to the beauty I saw in this woman.
I asked my friends for a leap of faith to help the woman.

Walking boldly to her table
I asked if I could photograph her
For a story about Saratoga
To appear in the Albany Times Union.

The spoon holding soup stopped
Her hand began to tremble
Shock, glimmering hope, disbelief, distrust
Combined in her eyes and face.
"Why photograph me?
I am old and ugly
Photograph others who are beautiful and wanted."

"Please, I begged.
"This young man is the writer
(Never mind he wrote only Sports)
This editor watches everything
I could be fired if you don't help me
(Never mind the Trial Attorney editor oddly kind for his breed of cat)

"I suppose so.
What do you want me to do?"

"Relax and be yourself.
I will do the rest."

I snapped her picture from every angle
Occasionally I guided her line of sight
Sometimes saying funny stuff
Getting different expressions.
Hugging her in thanks brought tears to my eyes.

As we left, I loudly said
"This is the centerpiece of the story."

From the car
I saw people hugging her,
Asking her questions,
Asking for her autograph.

Her life had changed
Perhaps for a moment
Perhaps for the rest of her life.

I do not know.
I never will.
Still I smile at the memory.

American City

My heart is a city

American city

Crannies of hurt

Nooks of memory

Neon lights of joy

Incomplete impressions

Kaleidoscopes

Sound and color

Moving shapes

Tugging, begging

Panhandling

To hold sway

In the stillness between

City heartbeats.

Relentless motion

Surging in love

Ebbing in fear

Sea of concrete

Chrome and steel

Shadowy caverns

Bottomless despair

Things unnamed
Done in the dark,
Skyscraping archways
Of circular highways
In and out
Breath and motion
Breath, emotion
Breath
       Heart
              City
American City.

'Nawlins (New Orleans)

Singing, chanting, swinging hips
Call-the-law music,
Fierce wildness
Of sticky swamps
Silent except slishes, sloshes
Of monstrous unseen
Slithering things.
Muddy, moldy, mildewed
Town
Seething, teeming
With riotous life.
Magic voodoo
Undulations
Undercurrents
To every breeze.

Saxophone wails
Rhythmic drums
Undertones to
Belching smokestacks
Police whistles

Siren emergencies
Drug-dealing
"Hey baby"
Street-corner greetings
Of the great, sprawling
Miasma - " 'Nawlins."

Debutantes of Audubon Park
Shrinks and shoppers
Maids and memberships
Marriages monetized
Maternities mandated.

Families
Living house-to-house
Generations
Cabdrivers, electricians, painters
Teachers, nurses, bums, deadbeats
Young girls to mothers too soon
Fighting
Politicians, poverty, hurricanes
Sharing
Money, food, time, love
Surviving
Doing the best they can.

Central Business District
Artificially clean
Stocks and bonds
Oil and gas
Land and water
People and profit
Futures and legacies.
Traded, dealt, conspired and willed.

History
Quadroon balls
Selecting a mistress
Slavery
Plantations and cotton
Mulatto children
Roaming streets
Searching for heritage

Always

Inevitably

The music

The musicians

In the Quarter –

Behind the strip clubs

Crowded streets of tourists

From everywhere, anywhere

The real American sound,

The Blues…

Sung, strummed, drummed, blown and keyed…

The constant welling

Of broken-hearted

Down-trodden

Helpless despair

Turned into a one-of-a-kind

Party that leaves no tomorrows

Erases yesterdays

Expands "right now" into

An endless string of

Gut-wrenching, soul-shattering

Notes

That stop time

Like a full-throttle freight train

Out of track

Falling into abyss
Of skin-crawling,
Heart-stopping
Fiery feeling.

Everything
All at once
That's 'Nawlins.
That's America.

New York City

Like a dewy-eyed girl
Fresh and full of marvel
In a purple sequined leotard
And pink ruffled tutu
Shiny black hoofer shoes
And a gold lame cane
Ready to Tap
        Strut
                Whirl
Through wind-tunnel streets

Wrapped in old quilting
Of her grandmother's stitching...

New York City.

West Texas Day

The West Texas sun
Claims the land
For its own
In the afternoons.
Cattle, men on horseback
Pedestrians, students,
Bums and welfare mothers
Slow to a crawl.
Artists flee indoors
Cool cafes and frothy mugs
Toasts and boasts
Of incomplete works.

Cooler evenings,
Families flip burgers
Fry beans and rice,
The lonely eat leftovers.

In the heart of the land,
Nocturnal creatures awaken,
Coyotes, mountain lions, bear
Raccoons, javelina and deer
Dance the dance of hunter and prey.
The night deepens,
Children sleeping
The vast, rugged terrain
Soaks the blood of nightly dead.

Mornings dawn
Pure and fresh,
Newborn rays
Welcome a day
Of promises kept
Hopes fulfilled
Unexpected magic.

The soul of the Earth
Is open here.
Come and live
West Texas days,
Come and breathe
The rarified air
Of angels, wolves and cowboys.

All You Have

I speak
Earth Mother's
Rage and tears
I am sent
To tell you
She cannot balance.
Killing cold
Stagnating, choking heat
Is all you have
Till, finally
You have only
Oceans with monstrous
Walls of water
Volcanic peaks
Constant eruption
Only that...
You are no more
Your children
Never are
Hang as shades
Unborn souls

No life

To inhabit.

Your future

Awaits.

A dim hope

Like palimpsest

Stop...

You already know

Stop

The toxins

Into your heart

A glimmer

Is all you have.

The Moment of America

I have driven the open roads
Of America.
Looking ahead
Great red rocks of the West,
The vast emptiness
Land loving itself
In beauty and strength.
Looking ahead
The highways
Looping, overlapping, stacking
Graceful curves
Of concrete and steel
Sculpted
By machines and imagination.

Looking ahead
Into the heart
Of dense, complicated
Eastern cities.

Ahead the future
Beautiful blank
Promise and fulfillment
Hope -
American hope
Better, brighter tomorrows.
Then…
A stop sign;
A turn?
Brakes and gas
A glance
In the rearview mirror

Behind –
Red rocks and wasted days
Dirty cities and broken dreams
Rearview welts
Of searing heartache
Fog cloying majestic landscape
Cloudy memories
Back alleys
Always dark
Drug deals
And cardboard condos

Secret loss
Hidden despair
In the past
Rearview only
Forgotten
In the blinding promise
Of tomorrow
The future
The open road.

Between the spotless future
And the sullied, already-lived past
The moment --
Open the door
Key in the ignition
Motor purring, growling, clattering
Seatbelt fastened
Tunes chosen
Freedom –
To choose the road
The moment -
The moment of hope
The moment of dream
The moment
Of America.

American People

OCAW

In cool darkness
Carved from heat
Of relentless sun,
Stench and smoke
From curving, rising
Pipelines of crude,
The dim bar lit
By Christmas lights
Twinkling mindlessly all year,
Sit laughing desperate men
Slurping suds of foam
From frosty mugs of ice-cold-beer.

Slapping backs in grateful play
For greasy, unionized
Soul-crushing, dirty work –
Deep
        Black
                Crude

Rising, bubbling
Through sand pits and pipes
Into keytone units
And tank farms.
In the few moments
Between work
And the crying, wanting
Sounds of home
"Where's the rent? Honey…?
Gulps of ice-cold frothy beer –
Survivorship.

Until the next
Breath of asbestos
Explosion of methane
Conflagration
A way of life.

Soldier's Poem

When I had sight
I saw flashing lights
Reflections, refractions
Slivers of image
Bits of shiny buttons
Golden braid
Synchopated white-gloved hands
Dismantling, assembling
Rifles, cannon, RPG's and MBT's.

When I had voice
I spoke in orders
"Yes sirs" and "copy that" codes,
Big, booming, bass baritone
Barbershop quartet voice
Laughing over "mess",
Sighing Saturday nights on R & R
Chanting Latin Sunday mornings
"Homne domine et Patri".

When I had hands
I made bunks
Cleaned latrines
Squeezed triggers
Staunched blood.

When I had legs
I strode the world
Proudly,
Confident in my country
My mastery
Of the arts of war
The love of peace
The tenderness
Of home and family,
"Cano armorum et homine."

I feel my hands…
Are they real?
Or memory?
Do I have legs?
No one touches me…
What is left of me?

I have Thoughts

        Memories

            Dreams

                Wonder

                    Curiosity…

Alone.
No way to reach
To say
I am here…
I am still here.

Strip Mall Improvisation

"Look," cried the child,

" A Dominoes. What's beside it?"

" A real estate office," Momma said.

" What's real estate?"

"A place to work for people who sell houses."

"What's beside that?"

" A mattress store that sells pillows and beds."

"And then?"

" A nail salon for fingers and toes,"

"Sells fingers and toes?"

Child curiosity creeping to fear…

" No, just shapes and paints and makes them pretty,"

"What's beside that?"

" I don't remember, " Momma laughed,

" We're a long way down the road."

" A dragon park," exclaimed the child

"What's a dragon park?"

Smiling Momma asked.

" A place where dragons play

While their Mommies' shop."

The child triumphant.

" Of course," Momma said.
" Can we make a story?"
The child eager,
"Can you begin?"

" Once upon a time,"
The piping, singsong voice began,
" A beautiful princess
In a far away land
Loved a golden dragon
With a curly tail and giant wings."
" Did the dragon have purple wings?'
Momma asked.
" No! The wings were red,
Now you, Momma."

"The beautiful princess
Flew her beloved dragon
To the nail salon'
The dragon played in the dragon park,"
"Yay! " cried the child.
" While the princess had a manicure."

"Then she went to the mattress store,"
Interrupted the child,
" To buy a bed for her dragon,
But the dragon
Wanted to go to the store, too,
So he flew through the door
Crashing the walls of the store.'
" Oh no," Momma feigning distress,
" What did the princess do?"
"She ordered Dominoes'
For everyone," shouted the child,
" And they all ate piazza together.
There's more, Momma,
While they were eating
A lady in the store
From the real estate office
Showed the princess pictures
Of a house next door to ours
They could buy
And have a place to sleep
When they come to visit.
The princess loved the house
And gave the lady
A big, shiny diamond for it."

" What a wonderful story," Momma said.
" How will we make stories
If all the malls were gone?"

"Don't worry,"
Momma said wryly,
" There will always be more strip malls."

A Different Day

"Today will be different"
A thought, a prayer
A million times repeated
Silent hope
Inspired by television
Pictures of families
Clean and safe
On fake sets
In air conditioned
Studios
Glimpses of "could be."
She stood
In warm rain
Steaming off summer streets
Nose pressed to fogged glass
Breathing
Just breathing
A long, slow moment
Escaping into circuitry
Endless images
Safe and bright and clean.

Reluctantly
Slowly
Like peeling
From the cool, unfeeling
Store front
Turning
Smiling
Slouching her hips
" Hey there Baby,
You looking for a date?"
Car door opening
Polished gun-metal gray
'I do a hand for 30
A blow for fifty and a..."
Too late -
Flash of silver blade
Missed her purse
Caught her chest
Blistering pain
Couldn't breathe
Out...out pushing
Running down the street
Wildly bleeding
Into the store
Falling, sobbing

Reaching
The TV families
Manager yelling
"Get out Get out
Not in here…Oh"

Calling 911
Sirens, lights

"Take it easy now."
"My baby,
my baby
she needs me…"
Seeing the tiny girl
Wrapped in a white blanket
Nestled in open drawer
Enfolding her
Whispering
"You're all right."

Hey Baby

Hey baby
Where ya goin?
Hey baby
Where ya been?
Life's a road to nowhere
Don't matter where you begin.

Hey baby
Whadda ya see?
Purple mountains majesty?
Amber waves of grain?
Probably not
Life's gone insane.

Ya see the river, baby?
Gold and blue
Keep lookin' at the river, baby
While your John's pumping you.
Never mind splinters in your back
Up against a wall
Backroom bar shack
Keep lookin' at the river, baby

Think of warm clothes
For your baby boys
Gloves, mittens
Christmas toys.

Hey baby
Where ya goin?
Hey baby
Where ya been?
Life's a road to nowhere
Don't matter where you begin.

Hey baby
Whadda ya see?
Purple mountains majesty?
Amber waves of grain?
Probably not
Life's gone insane.

Wash up in the ladies room
Hair smooth in a bun
You look like anybody
Out for a run.

Grab a beer in the bar
A little bubbling cheer
While you're gulping
You catch the next guy's leer.

Hey baby
Where ya goin?
Hey baby
Where ya been?
Life's a road to nowhere
Don't matter where you begin.

Hey baby
Whadda ya see?
Purple mountains majesty?
Amber waves of grain?
Probably not
Life's gone insane.

Knuckles and Bone

When it gets down

To knuckles and bone

Yardlines in sandlot

Blurred by rain

Teams erased in mud

Only bodies moving

Muscles surging -

Relentless indomitable play

Of balls and nerve.

This is football.

This is America…

Not the glory dogs

Of yards per play

Plays per games

Games per injuries

Injuries per death…

Just play

In the mud

At midnight

Exulting…

Strength nothing can touch

American.
Power increasing
With each
Jaunty, rakish careless
Wave, stride, grin
Thoughtless might
Present action
Fearlessness.
Completely alive
In crushing abandon
The American message -

"Fear me because
I Fear Nothing!
We who are about to win
Accept your cheers."

Robo Wolf

Raindrops and sirens
American song
Long, wailing cop-car cry
Like Robo Wolf…
Mechanized Roamer
Hunting, sniffing
Seeking the weak and hurt
Needing quick death
Or paramedics.

Nexus of Hearts

Tonight I watched
Boxing on television…
Great acting
Cinematography like genius
I saw my country
With new eyes.
Metaphor more than real
Every punch landed
Breaking rib
Snapped jaw
Bloody, spilling eye cut
Performing turned to competition
Competition to intimacy
Vulnerability to respect
With each blow, groan, bruise and tear.
America is not easy
America cuts and bloodies
Dark, ominous countenance
Smiling wreathes of rainbows
Everything in between
Intensely alive

A hum in God's ear

A curve 'round Earth's hip

America –

Nexus of hearts

Matrix of souls

Defining our time.

Street Prophets

You find them

In Times Square

The French Quarter

Chicago's Rush Street

Underground Atlanta

LA streetcorner

Angels,

Prophets,

Insane,

Psychotic,

Holy,

Overlords

In a land

All their own

We look - wondering

        Longing

            Frightened

                Unsettled

By the inside out

World oracles trod
Arms outstretched
Hands beseeching
Palms up
Words flowing
Uncensored.

We scoff them off
As mad
We see them
Casually shrugging
Out of social context
Like too tight leather
We turn from their
Vehemence, passion
Reassured by their rags
Dirt, smell, utter disregard
For what we kill for
And yet...

As we turn away
Chilled
Disturbed
In deep, subterranean
Places

Chords of truth
Resonate
Shivering, we pause, listen
Move on- shaken

We stop at a bar
Order a double
Slug it back
Paste on a smile
Swagger down a street
But...
We know the swagger
Know the paste
We know...

Monarchs of the Drivers' Seat

We delight in the FLASH -
SNAP – CRACKLE – POP
Of the open road.
Touring in our cars
"Candy-colored, tangerine-flake,
Stream-lined" babies,
Sleek cadillacs,
Beamers, Jaguars, Chevys
Unabashed, big-bellied V-8s
Purring, growling, horse-power.
Tiny toot-toots from hybrid Minis
Like striped tuna cans
Boring, boxy family cars
Dramatic, winged Lamborghini
Pegasus of the parkway
High finned, patch worked, low-ryders
Circling like sharks.
In our cars
We belong to ourselves
No neighborhood, social class,
We are sovereign states.

Mobile, motorized
Monarchs of the driver's seat.
Oracles of the open road,
Billboards our bible
Golden arches our sanctuary.
Freedom, possibility
Just over the next hill.
A car
Good suite of clothes
Couple a bucks
For gas and a burger,
We are free
To be anybody
Living any life
American.

Privileges of Citizenship

We are here

In cubes, logged on

Waiting

For calls from the sick, frightened, old

Grasping, poor

Americans

Wanting

A slice of the pie

A piece of the Dream

Grateful for the crumbs

Of Public Health

A brief, sugared moment

On the phone

With a stranger

Getting respect and dignity

As a citizen

In those sweet fragments

Of conversation

With a Call Center rep

Making thirty a year

Feeling safe with a job

To pay the rent
For the run-down apartment
With the leaky hot water
And huge electric bill.
Privileges of citizenship.

Kidz

Behold the American "kidz…"
A new breed
Strong, questing
Questioning
Laughing at limits…
Playful adults
Wisdom's children…

Heads thrown back
Strong shoulders shrugging
Sardonic grin
Unruly hair everywhere
"Look at me
I am new
I rule the world."

Oozing carelessness
In their Dancing
      Side-stepping
           Sway…
Kidz born in motion

Easy grace

Iconoclastic

Curling vaping smoke framing

All-knowing grin

Live for today

Convenient mantra

Boundless exuberance

Singing

    Lurching

Come-what-may

Rhythmns

Of fearless exploration

    Mind

        Heart

            Spirit

                World

                    Universe

Behold the American kidz

Future back-spaced

Only the now.

Sunday Night Blues

It's that feeling
Oh yeah, that crazy feeling
Kinda blue kinda sad
Kinda eager kinda mad
Weekend is over
Was it fun?
Was it enough?
Can't stop the clock
Sunday clicks away
Monday comes in strong
Life is just a tick tock
A breath by breath song.

We are American

We are constantly moving
We jet and drive and cab and bus,
We hop a train
Bum a ride
Walk the city streets
Pausing in doorways
Crumbling apartment buildings
Chatting with teen-age mothers
Unemployed fathers.

We walk to a subway station
Ride uptown
To chrome and glass office,
We sign the deals
Try the cases
Creating absent landlords
Absent parents
Too tired
From working too long
For too little.
Rent is late

Supper is skimpy
Hungry children
Dream of burgers and biscuits.
We tuck the babies
Into make-shift stroller
Walking streets, boulevards, highways
To welfare office, free clinic, food pantry, jail.

We bundle the family
Into town car service
To the airport,
The long flight
Cranky squabbling
Soothed with ipad games
Papaya smoothies,
Then – bursting
Into sunlit, balmy, beach-play,
Vacation.
Parasailing, snorkeling, surfing
Dancing, dining
On lobster and key lime pie.
Returning home
To leave again
For work, play, school, library, movie…

We walk, run, ramble
Move up, down, over
"Onward and upward"
Believing in a brighter future,
Behind us
The long, grey line
Those left behind
Ahead rejoicing faces
Of the rescued few.
We move on…
We are American.

American Soul

American Dream

I hear America wailing
The cry of a mother
Over her son,
A young black man
Shot in the back
By police,
Bleeding in the street
Spectators videoing murder.

I hear America gasping
Choking on the refuse
Of smoking refineries,
Wheezing atmosphere
Laden with planes
Whooshing…
Passengers in constant motion
Willy Nilly…
Across the wrecked and torn skies.

I hear America pleading
The dirty, stained faces of children
Tasting a hot breakfast
In an institutional cafeteria
Their wide-eyed chortles
A plea for the egalitarian
Promise
Of America.

I breathe America hoping,
In the fading
Light of day
In the purple haze
Of night approaching
The embrace of sky and earth
In night's sweet slumber,
The dream of you
The dream of me
American
Awaking strong.

We sleep entwined
Dreaming
A day of days
Of joy and love
And full-bellied laughter
We dream.

I hear America dreaming
The dream of hope.

America Dreaming

I feel America dreaming
Down deep
In the gut, heart, soul
A Dream of Better
A dream imbedded
In the American essence
A dream becoming
Rock, dirt, water, grain, flesh
A dream --becoming
Faces west
Toward a shining future
Muddling through becomes heroic
Suffering becomes meaningful
Endurance key to the Promised Land.

I feel America dreaming
In spite of
War
       Slaughter
              Pain
                     Terror

Crime

    Rape

        Bigotry

            Racism

I feel America dreaming
The dream of freedom
The dream of hope
Dreaming for the world

Light and beacon
Pathway to better
Gilding the present
With shining future
To be American
Is to Feel America Dreaming.

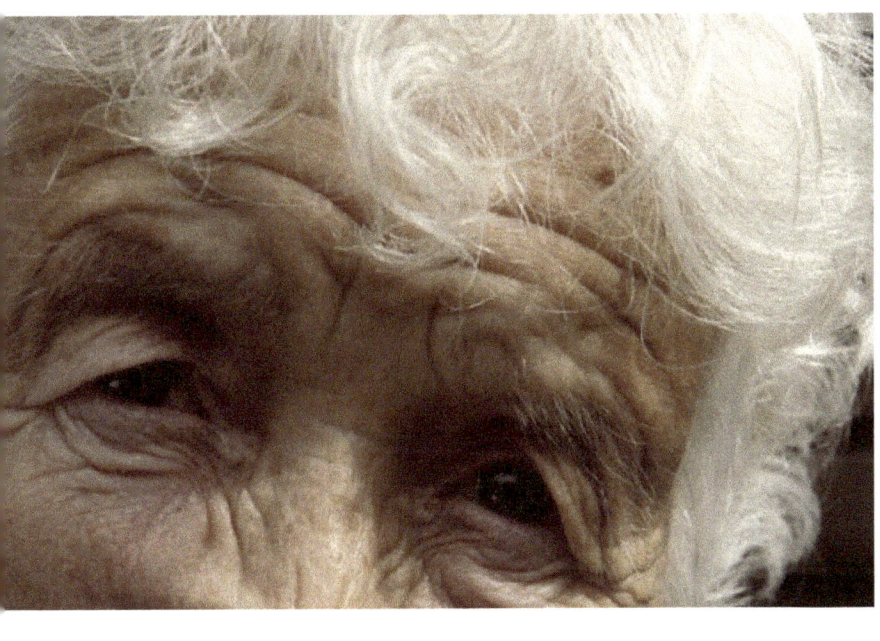

American Spirits

I am your future

My hot, young American.

Do not look

To your children

You love them

Suffer their loss

As they grow

As they forget you.

Look instead

At my bright eye

My Strength

      Wisdom

           Power

I am Age

I am experience

I am maturity.

I see your

Desperate struggles

As amusement

You do not know

What lies ahead
Only I know -
Life breaks you
Six ways from Sunday
You are destined
To shatter and mend
And go on…
Many devastations
Before you are strong
Like ancient, blasted rocks
Of the great Salt Lake
The crushed Texas coast
After a hurricane.

Look to me...
I am your promise
Your future
Listen to me.

Vibrancy
Animation
Housed in
Stooped
Weathered
Frames

Youth is illusion.
Unformed energy
Like embryo sacks
Of potential.
Nothing more.

Seek the aged
For guidance
We are the signposts,
Our power
Holds the earth
Together
Letting life be.

If you want
A world
After you are gone
Harness us
Ask us
Cherish us
We are your
Future,
We are your
Inevitability
We have been

Obliterated
And rebirthed ourselves
Like mighty Titans
Enormous
Striding the Earth
Like a playground
Mountain ranges
Toy blocks
To our mighty thighs.

Take heed of us
We are the
Old
      Stooped
             Wrinkled
Powerhouses -
American Spirits
Incarnate.

Balancing – City on a Hille

The City on the Hille
Shining beacon
Eternal hope
Proof in the pudding
Freedom.
The awful bliss to choose
What to do
Where to go
How to live
Dream sequence
Called life
In America
Always a balancing act
Tiptoe across a tight wire,

Freedom one end
Order the other
Power exuding
Walkers -

Nonchalant

Happily texting

Unaware

Indifferent

To the abyss below.

Balancing

The American Way

Balancing…

From Whence We Came

We sing the song of ourselves
In every breath, spin, smile, hug, push
Shout, laugh, cry, whisper
A song of the soul
A song of the flesh
A song of the spirit eternal
A song rooted in time and place
Captured in personality
Limited by geography
We sing an endless lament
Of definition
A song of longing
For the infinite unknowable
We are sister, brother, daughter,
Wife, husband, son
American
Made grand by history
Given a glimpse of the Promised Land

Always travelling
Reaching
To write, paint, sing
Dance, play or buy
That place…
The confluence of being
From whence we came.

I Am My Own Country

I am my own country
Walking sacred earth
Lightly
      Gently
            Gracefully

With purpose and strength
Enduring…
I am my own country
Speaking music
Syllables rounded
Languages bridge to all
I am my country
And all are in my country
I am my own country
Customs, heritage, nationality
Artificial demarcations
Relics that can enrich
But cannot divide
I am my own country.
You call me
America.

Strength of Your Muscles

I am the strength of your muscles

I am the light of your eyes

I am the blood-soaked power

Of your endurance

I am the limitless measure

Of your resolve.

I am the land of your

Fathers and Mothers

I am the place

You begin

You call home

You return

Your final dust becomes

My soil.

I am America.

Color Song

Sing of me
I am the Land
Your "sea to shining sea"
Effervescing streams
Laughing wild
Gleeful tumbling
To rivers – wide and slow
Sweeping strong currents
Life-blood
To my valleys and plains.

Mountains of me
Pushing outward
Into Sky
Reaching for sun
Tickling trees
Laughing ocean spray.

Depths of me
Shadowy caverns
Subterranean
Watery catacombs
Ancient currents
Swell and recede
In me.

Delicate glistening
Dewdrops of morning
On butterfly wings
Lightest breath
Ruffling baby's hair
Cherishing.

I am your spine
The bone of your resolve
Breathe me in
I fill your lungs
I am your arrogance
Your pride…
You flourish
In my patience
You thrive
On my forbearance.

Sing of me
Sing my screams echoing
In Arizona copper mines
In Colorado railroad tunnels
Dead rivers devoid of oxygen…
Hear my laments
In your coughs and gasps
Of your sickened lungs
Weakened hearts.

Chorus with me
Through my glorious autumn
My trees
Singing their color song
Sing of me
I am your majestic past
Hopeful future…
I am
Blood, bone, fire
In your belly…
I am your laugh
Your shining eyes
Your power;
I am your dreams.
I am you

You are me

I am America

You are Americans.

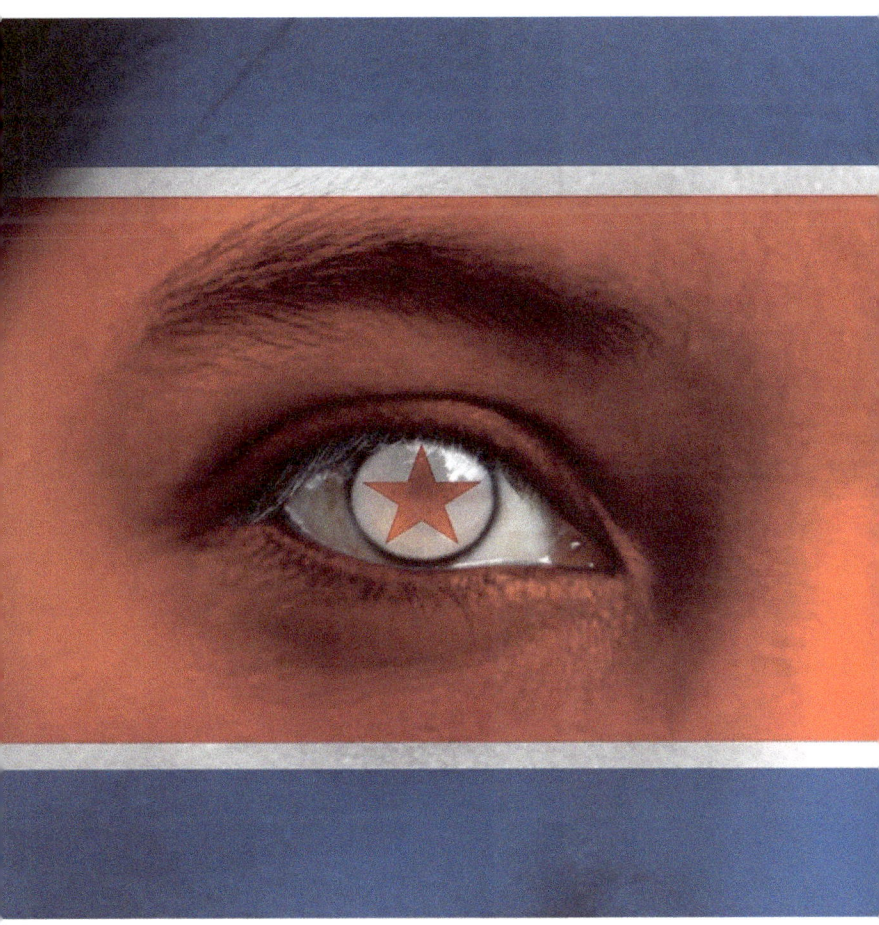

Mine Eyes Have Seen

1957

Ravaged town
Audrey made landfall
Cat 4 storm
Coloring windows
Purple and white
Thunder
Like the end of the world
No water, no lights
Floodwaters
Rushing past doors
"Mommy...
Can we go swimming?"
Trips to the water wagon
Drinking water
Damp washcloth
For a bath
Canned food
Like a picnic
Hot...

Sweaty, sticky
Water receding
Sun blasting
Dead things
Everywhere…

1963

Fifth grade recess
Shouting
Like kids do
The President is shot
The President is shot
Teachers in tears
Parents in tears
Scary big tears
On adult faces
Learning solemnity
First time tragedy
For most of us…
Knowing only
A different kind of bad
Something
So huge
The world stopped

Like breathless alone
In the dark.

1966

The shooting
Sniper atop the tower
UT Austin
43 dead
The world knew
Murder
In a new way
Mass murder
Public places
Military
"Execellent Marine"
Trauma
Head searing
Fingers on trigger
Squeezing, squeezing
Till police bullets hit home
Hit America's finest...
Survivors changed forever
Now carrying the trauma
He sought to discharge

With rifle rounds
50 years
Till we learned
The healing
Of grieving
Reflection pool built…
Mass shootings
New warfare
Terrorism
Not yet
Depraved Monsters
Slaughtering Innocents
Bizzare
    Twisted
        Idealism....

1969

"...One giant leap
For mankind..."
Watching in wonder
Walking the moon
Images on TV
The world smaller
Imagination expanded

Armstrong thinking
Knowing he held
Moment of History
What words would do?
Immortal words
Symbolic words
Hope
A better tomorrow
American hope
American Dream
Made real
Power of Image
Television
And a Distant Moon.

Distant jungle
Fiery orange
Rat a tat tat
Woop woop woop
Helicopters
Body bags
Napalm
"Good Morning Vietnam"
Rice paddies
Red with blood

Questioning

        Questioning…

The generation

That questioned

Protested

War, racism

National Guard

Killing students

Demonstrators

Kent State

Revolution

Defining the future

Reweaving

Social fabric

Closing the gap

Bleeding

        Singing,

                Wailing…

American Dream to

American Reality.

The chants continue…

The march continues…

The human spirit
Longing to be free
Hope embodied
America.

1980's

Then
There's Wall street
Another bloody jungle
Educated
Ivy League
Criminals
Crushing spirit
Sucking life
Squashing hope
Through swaps
Deriviatives
Chortling
To the bank
Saying "for the kids.."
Thinking "they're safe.."
Saved from torment
By blood money
Children grown

Despising
Swaddling life
Turning to action
Grit of desert
Afganhanstan
Iraq
More body bags
Broken hearts
Blood to ashes
Ashes to dust
Dust to dust
Criminals
Still free
Still squeezing
Hands grimy
Souls stained
Vampires
Without glamor
No immortality
Just baggy eyes
Vacant stares
All light gone...

1992-1999

Koresh, Bobbitt
OJ Simpson
Timothy McVeigh
JonBenet Ramsey
Dolly
Tiger Woods
Bill Clinton
Viagra
Hits the market.
America splintering.

Flashes of news stories
Glimpses through airports
Late night TV
Falling asleep
In another strange hotel
Chasing career
Making money
Like it was immortality.

2001

In my office
Television news
In the background
Busy day
Calls to make
Gigs to get …

"Have reports of a plane
Hitting the World Trade Center,"

Looking casually
Over my shoulder
Calls to make
Gigs to get…

"Not a small plane
Airliner full of passengers
Perhaps an act of terror."
Stopped to listen…but
Calls to make

Gigs to get

"A second airliner
Heading for Building Two
World Trade Center."

Stopped.

Compelled to watch -
World watching too

When the second tower fell

Crumbling, crushing, fiery

Collapse…

Bodies falling from windows

Enormous glass and steel

Swaying…

A willow in a windstorm

Graceful, surreal implosion

Cameras rolling

Street view

All roaring thunder

Tsunami of black smoke

Shattering glass

Engulfing

Force of the final fall

Ripping, tearing

Spilling the guts

Of Lower Manhattan

Of America.

Together
Watching, weeping, mourning
Healing…
Forever changed.
One short, sunny morning
Like any other
From : "Horrible accident…"
To shock, disbelief, Terror…
Terror…
The New Enemy…
Upsurge of patriotism
International empathy
Months of flag-waving,
Singing, vigils for the dead, lost,
Wandering…
Workmen losing lungs
At Ground Zero
Handling remains reverently
Giving their bodies recovering others.

Rage sweeping America
A windstorm outraging
Terror enraging
Swelling to vengeance
Shock and Awe…

The MOAB's fell
Fissuring the cracked, blackened
Despairing landscape
Poisoned with land mines
Claiming limbs
Lifetime of war
Becoming destiny itself
Afganistan.
Then Iraq
Weapons of Mass Destruction
Supposedly…
Deadly, deadly blunder.

America blushed
Applause of the world
Squandered
In air strikes continuing
Ground troops returning
Twisted, maimed bodies
Tormented spirits
Fighting the blood lust of war
With lawn mowers
Kids' birthday parties
Corporate paychecks
Family vacations…

2008

Economic collapse!
"Too big to fail."
Big banks bailed
Tax money turned
Executive bonuses
Robber Barons
Given big money
From little people
Bloody faces
Smearing American Pie.

2012

Technology!
Information age!
Mobile devices abound
Access to infinite knowledge
Bank accounts, groceries, birthdays,
Headlines, horoscopes, bills…
Videos, photos,
Emails, voice mails, texts…
In a pocket-sized, battery charged
Glitzy, crazy-colored, slip-in-a-pocket
Personal window
To the new New World;
Enveloping, enfolding
Embracing, entertaining
As exhilarating
Horrifying, uplifting and tragic
As anything in real life.

Give me my apps!
Demands the Techno Generations
All ages welcome!
Give me maximum speed
Super-power operating system
GPS, USB 3.0 and Flash Drives
All the cuddling, cradling, sexy
Recombinant
Apps in our DNA.
American landscape
Beyond sea to shining sea
Now everywhere, nowhere
In cyberspace.

2017

The American Woman
Strange creatures…
As a girl, feeling my mother's anguish
Watching her fight for respectability
Viewed skeptically by "polite society"
Divorced with children
My pious, tee totaling mother
Labelled "light – heeled"
Rigid, conformist culture.

I was young

Motherhood sanctioned by marriage

A mandate;

Career? A fall-back plan …

Out of wedlock?

Have a scarlet A,

Wear it on your chest.

Now…

"Wanna have a baby

Before the wedding

Don't wanna be

Pregnant in pictures…"

"Baby? Aw not now…"

"Children? Maybe later

Just got a job…"

Just got a promotion

Just started a business

Just made CEO

Just got published

Just got elected…

Breaking bonds

Doors

        Glass ceilings…

Ascendancy of the female

Fulfilling historical promise

American woman

Fiercely independent

Wicked smart

Walking

    Swaggering

        Dancing

A new road

For Self

    Country

        World

God shed her grace on thee…
America the Beautiful.

Epilogue
Life in the Time of Pandemic

Listening…
Newstories terrifying
Deaths accelerating
National dialogue
"Who to let die?"
Social media
Lifeline connections
Am I becoming Millennial?

Not a chance!
I still believe
Long walks, deep meditations
Chocolate and diamonds
Lots of doggie kisses
And a better tomorrow.

I am American.